MYTHS UNDERSTOOD

UNDERSTANDING MESOAMERICAN MYTHS

NATALIE HYDE

 Crabtree Publishing Company

www.crabtreebooks.com

Author: Natalie Hyde
Publishing plan research and development:
  Sean Charlebois, Reagan Miller
  Crabtree Publishing Company
Editor-in-chief: Lionel Bender
Editors: Simon Adams, Lynn Peppas
Proofreaders: Laura Booth, Kathy Middleton
Photo research: Kim Richardson
Designer: Ben White
Cover design: Margaret Amy Salter
Production coordinator and Prepress technician:
  Samara Parent
Production: Kim Richardson
Print coordinator: Katherine Berti

Consultants: Amy Leggett-Caldera, M.Ed., Elementary
and Middle School Education Consultant, Mississippi
State University.

Cover: Human skull (middle center); Boa Constrictor
(bottom left); Jaguar (bottom right); Aztec calendar stone
(bottom middle); Chichen Itza Modern Seven Wonders
of the World in Mexico (middle top); gods Quetzalcoatl
and Tezcatlipoca (top left and right)

Title page: The Ancient Mayan Ruins of Tikal
in Guatemala

Photographs and reproductions:
Cover: Thinkstock (bottom right, middle center, bottom left and right,
middle top); Wikimedia Commons: (top left and right); El
Comandante: (bottom middle)
Maps: Stefan Chabluk
shutterstock.com: 1 (ClimberJAK), 4t (lrafael), 5 (Vladimir
Korostyshevskiy), 6t (Hannah Gleghorn), 12–13 (Vadim Petrakov), 16t
(lrafael), 20 (Marco Regalia), 24t (Nino Cavalier), 34t (Elena Fernandez
Zabelguelskaya), 36l (sursad), 36r (Kitch Bain), 40 (W. Scott), 40–41
(Kate Connes), 44b (aquatic creature)
Topfoto (EE Images/HIP): 14; (The Granger Collection): 11, 16b, 21,
24b, 25, 31, 34b, 35, 38, 39, 42; (Imageworks): 26, 43; (Paul Ross): 37;
(Topfoto): 44t; (World History Archive): 15, 22, 30
Werner Forman Archive: 4b (Biblioteca Universitaria, Bologna, Italy),
6b (British Museum, London), 9t (Subbotina Anna), 9b (Francisco
Caravana), 10t (W. Scott), 10b (Private Collection), 12, 17 (St Louis Art
Museum, Mo.), 18 (N.J. Saunders), 19 (Private Collection, New York),
23 (Museum fur Volkerkunde, Basel, Switzerland), 27 (Museum of
Americas, Madrid), 28 (N.J. Saunders), 29 (National Museum of
Anthropology, Mexico City), 32 (Museum of Americas, Madrid)

This book was produced for Crabtree Publishing Company
by Bender Richardson White

Library and Archives Canada Cataloguing in Publication

Hyde, Natalie, 1963-
Understanding Mesoamerican myths / Natalie Hyde.

(Myths understood)
Includes index.
Issued also in electronic formats.
ISBN 978-0-7787-4525-9 (bound).--ISBN 978-0-7787-4530-3 (pbk.)

1. Indian mythology--Central America--Juvenile literature.
2. Indians of Central America--Religion--Juvenile literature.
I. Title. II. Series: Myths understood

F1434.2.R3H93 2012   j299.7'92   C2012-906838-1

Library of Congress Cataloging-in-Publication Data

Hyde, Natalie, 1963-
  Understanding Mesoamerican myths / Natalie Hyde.
      p. cm. -- (Myths understood)
  Includes index.
  ISBN 978-0-7787-4525-9 (reinforced library binding) -- ISBN
978-0-7787-4530-3 (pbk.) -- ISBN 978-1-4271-9059-8 (electronic
(pdf)) -- ISBN 978-1-4271-9113-7 (electronic (html))
  1. Aztec mythology--Juvenile literature. 2. Maya mythology
--Juvenile literature. 3. Indian mythology--Juvenile
literature. I. Title.

  F1219.76.R45H94 2013
  299.7'92--dc23
                                    2012040536

Crabtree Publishing Company

www.crabtreebooks.com   1-800-387-7650

Printed in the U.S.A./112012/FA20121012

Published in Canada
Crabtree Publishing
616 Welland Ave.
St. Catharines, Ontario
L2M 5V6

Published in the United States
Crabtree Publishing
PMB 59051
350 Fifth Avenue, 59th Floor
New York, New York 10118

Published in the United Kingdom
Crabtree Publishing
Maritime House
Basin Road North, Hove
BN41 1WR

Published in Australia
Crabtree Publishing
3 Charles Street
Coburg North
VIC 3058

CONTENTS

WHAT ARE MYTHS?

Ancient cultures from around the world influence our daily lives. The way ancient peoples built their cities, the festivals they celebrated, and their methods of farming and hunting can still be found in our society today.

Some ancient cultures did not have a written language so they passed on their knowledge and beliefs in their stories. Through fables, legends, and myths, they were able to teach the next generation.

Fables are a type of story that teach a lesson. Legends are historical stories based on some true facts. Myths tell of gods, magic, and strange creatures. Myths are the stories of a culture's beliefs. They help to explain how the world was created, how it works, and how humans survive.

These myths were recorded in ancient books, **scrolls**, or on tablets. They were also passed down from one generation to another as spoken tales. Myths are shown in drawings, sculptures, and carvings.

Right: The god of darkness gives offerings before a temple in ancient Mexico in which an owl, the symbol of total destruction, lived.

THE OLMEC GODS

The oldest myths in Mesoamerica belonged to the Olmec people. Statues and carvings show images of eight different gods: the Olmec Dragon, the Maize God, the Bird Monster, the Were-Jaguar, the Rain Spirit, the Banded-eye God, the Feathered Serpent, and the Shark Monster.

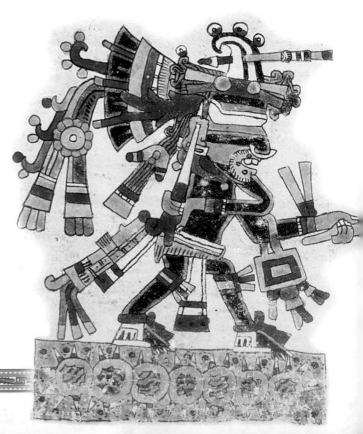

THE JAGUAR

In Olmec sculptures, jaguars are not often shown as just a wild animal. They are shown as half human and half big cat. Some figures are shown crouching, as if ready to change from one to the other.

LINK TO TODAY

Guatemalan worry dolls are said to take your worries and hold them so you can sleep. This is based on an ancient Mesoamerican tradition in which amulets, jewelry, or small ornaments could take away your fears or anxiety.

Left: An Aztec dancer performs at the New York American Indian Festival in Brooklyn, in 2010.

ANCIENT MESOAMERICA

Mesoamerica means middle America and includes the region from today's central Mexico south through Guatemala, Belize, El Salvador, Honduras, and Nicaragua into northern Costa Rica. Even though there were many tribes living in the area, they shared many things such as their mythology, religion, style of buildings, ball games, and use of calendars.

The region has two very different landscapes: the lowlands and the highlands. Ancient peoples living in the lowlands had a **tropical** climate with warm temperatures year round. The rain forests in the lowlands provided a good source of food, although farming was difficult. People who lived in the highlands endured a much drier and colder climate. Growing crops was a challenge because the soil was poor and the weather was harsh.

Most of Mesoamerica is crisscrossed by rivers. This water was vital for drinking, watering crops, and transportation through the rain forest. Water was very

Above: This mask is thought to represent the god Quetzalcoatl, although it could be a representation of Tonatiuh, the Sun god. On the death of a king, masks were placed on the dead person's face.

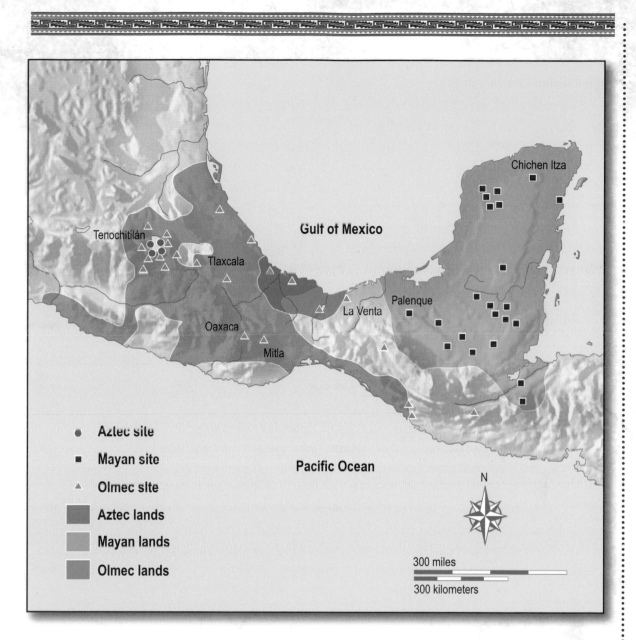

Map legend:
- Aztec site (●)
- Mayan site (■)
- Olmec site (▲)
- Aztec lands
- Mayan lands
- Olmec lands

Map labels: Chichen Itza, Tenochitilán, Tlaxcala, Gulf of Mexico, Palenque, La Venta, Oaxaca, Mitla, Pacific Ocean

300 miles
300 kilometers

important and there were different gods and goddesses for lakes, rivers, storms, and oceans. The goddess Chalchiutlicue ruled over lakes and streams and brought water for the crops, but she could be vengeful, too. She brought storms to drown the world.

Chalchiutlicue's name means "She who wears a **jade**, or green, skirt." She was the water goddess who also symbolized youth and beauty. She was the wife of Tlaloc, the rain god, and together they ruled the kingdom of Tlalocan, which was one of the levels of heaven. According to myth, she released 52 years of rain on Earth.

Above: The three main cultures in Mesoamerica were the Aztec culture in what is now Mexico in the north, the Olmec in the center, and the Maya in the east on the Yucatan peninsula.

TYPES OF MYTHS

The people of Mesoamerica used myths to explain why their world looked and worked the way it did. Creation myths helped them to understand how Earth and all the living things on it were created. The volcanoes and mountains in these regions were described in landscape myths. Destructive earthquakes, floods, **droughts**, and violent tropical storms were thought to be caused by angry gods and were described in numerous nature myths.

These myths also showed the qualities that Mesoamerican people valued. With invaders always threatening their way of life, they admired anyone who could outsmart an enemy. They believed that trickery was not a bad trait when it was used against a foe.

Sacrifice was a common theme in Mesoamerican myths. It was considered noble to give up your crops, animals, or even human life if it would help others live and prosper by keeping the gods happy.

THE HERO TWINS TRICK THE LORDS OF DEATH

Mesoamericans created many myths about the struggles of life and death. Most of them involved tests of strength and willpower.

The Lords of Death liked to trick people into dying and coming to live with them in the **underworld**. These unlucky humans included Hun Hunuaphu and his brother. But Hun Hunuaphu had twin sons who were very clever. They went to see the Lords of Death to avenge their father's and uncle's deaths.

The twins, Hunuaphu and Xbalanque, knew that the first test was to call the gods by their names. They made a mosquito out of hair and it flew into the underworld first. When it bit one of the gods, the other gods called out its name to ask what was the matter. After each god was bitten, the twins knew all of their names and greeted them properly.

Then the gods asked Hunuaphu and Xbalanque to sit down. The twins remembered the story of their father who was burned as he sat on a bench, so they refused. The Lords of Death were frustrated. They wanted to find a way to kill the twins. So they sent them to three houses to be tested further. The twins were not tricked and beat the Lords of Death.

THE DOORWAY

A cenote was a deep well that formed naturally in **limestone** and was thought to be a doorway to the gods. In rituals, or ceremonies, to bring rain, sacrifices were thrown down the sacred cenote at Chichen Itza for Chac, the rain god.

Right: This cenote in Chichen Itza in Mexico is called Ik-Kil.

Below: Kukulkan is a traditional Mayan temple pyramid in Chichen Itza.

RELIGION *AND* GODS

All Mesoamerican cultures, including the Olmec, Mayan, and Aztec, believed in polytheism, meaning they believed in more than one god. Each god or goddess had a role caring for or controlling different parts of the world.

The Olmecs, one of the oldest cultures of Mesoamerica, had at least eight gods. The Maya adopted some of these earlier gods and myths, and folded them into their own pantheon, or group of gods. The Aztecs did the same, changing names and adding to the Mayan gods but keeping many of the same myths and mythic heroes. For example, the Feathered Serpent was worshiped by the Olmecs. The Maya called him Kukulkan, and later the Aztecs called him Quetzalcoatl.

Mesoamericans did not see their gods as only good or bad. Most gods could have a **dual** nature, helping humankind when they were happy or causing destruction and misery when they were angry.

Right: God K, the god of lightning identified by the torch running through his forehead, is one of three lightning gods who created Earth and its animals.

BOOK OF THE PEOPLE

The book *Popol Vuh*, or *"Book of the People,"* is the earliest collection of Mesoamerican myths ever found. They were first written down by a Dominican priest named Father Francisco Ximénez while he worked in Guatemala in the 1700s.

TLALOC, THE GOD OF RAIN, THUNDER, AND LIGHTNING

Tlaloc was a good example of the dual personality of many of the Aztec gods. As the god of rain, he could send life-giving rain to the crops. But, if angered, he could send something much worse.

Tlaloc carried four jugs with him. One jug contained rain. When he poured from this jug, the crops were watered and grew. If he forgot to send rain, sometimes a sacrifice would remind him.

In a second jug, Tlaloc had drought. This dried up the rivers and streams and could bring **starvation**.

In a third jug was frost. If Tlaloc was angered, he could send a late frost to the tender new plants and cause them to blacken and die.

In the fourth jug was disease. Illnesses that the Aztecs thought dangerous, including **leprosy,** were passed along in water.

If Tlaloc banged his jugs together, they would cause thunder and lightning. Tlaloc ruled in the kingdom of Tlalocan, where people who drowned or died of diseases carried by water would live with him, surrounded by beautiful flowers and flowing rivers.

Right: Tlaloc, the Aztec god of water and rain, could be kind in his actions or cruel.

GODS OF CREATION

For the Maya and Aztecs of Mesoamerica, Earth was a living being. It was created on the back of a reptile. Above it were the layers of the sky and below it were the layers of the underworld.

The Mesoamericans believed that heaven was divided into 13 layers. Each layer was ruled over by one or more gods.

Both the Maya and Aztecs believed that the newly dead had to travel through some terrible places to reach their place of rest. Rivers of scorpions and blood, mountains crashing into one another, and fierce jaguars were the types of tests humans had to overcome on their final journey.

Mesoamericans believed that the heavens, Earth, and underworld were joined together by the Tree of Life. This massive tree had roots in the underworld and its trunk in the physical world, while its highest branches reached the heavens. This was how humankind traveled from one layer to another.

Center: The frill on the top of the pyramid at Palenque in Mexico might represent thunder.

Right: It has been suggested that the stone in front of the Palace of the Governors at Uxmal in Mexico is a representation of the Tree of Life.

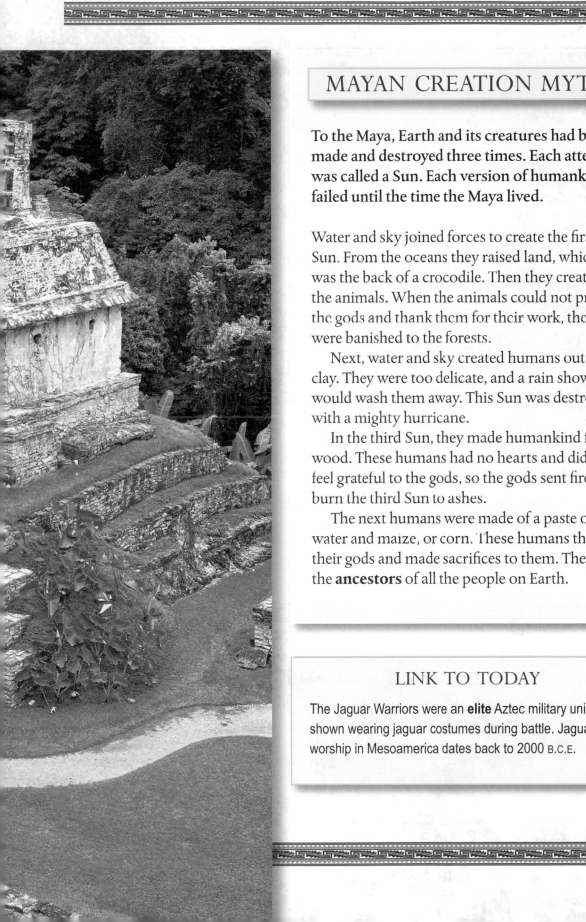

MAYAN CREATION MYTH

To the Maya, Earth and its creatures had been made and destroyed three times. Each attempt was called a Sun. Each version of humankind failed until the time the Maya lived.

Water and sky joined forces to create the first Sun. From the oceans they raised land, which was the back of a crocodile. Then they created all the animals. When the animals could not praise the gods and thank them for their work, they were banished to the forests.

Next, water and sky created humans out of clay. They were too delicate, and a rain shower would wash them away. This Sun was destroyed with a mighty hurricane.

In the third Sun, they made humankind from wood. These humans had no hearts and did not feel grateful to the gods, so the gods sent fire to burn the third Sun to ashes.

The next humans were made of a paste of water and maize, or corn. These humans thanked their gods and made sacrifices to them. They are the **ancestors** of all the people on Earth.

LINK TO TODAY

The Jaguar Warriors were an **elite** Aztec military unit, often shown wearing jaguar costumes during battle. Jaguar worship in Mesoamerica dates back to 2000 B.C.E.

MORTALITY AND DEATH

In Mesoamerican cultures death was not seen as the end of life but part of a continuing cycle. They believed that death gave life by giving the gods their energy and allowing it to be used to create new life.

Mesoamericans believed that some ways of dying were nobler than others. Depending on how a person died, he or she would go to a different level of heaven or the underworld. People who died by drowning or diseases linked with water, such as leprosy, went to spend eternity with the rain god. Those who died by **suicide** or sacrifice went straight to the highest level of heaven. To prepare a body for burial, Mayan and Aztec people would wrap the body in cotton cloth. The Maya would place some maize in the mouths of the dead so they would have food on their long journey. They would also place a piece of jade in their mouths to pay the toll, or fee through the underworld.

The Maya buried their dead, often under their houses. Aztecs often **cremated** the dead and kept the ashes in pots.

Below: These elaborate stone carvings from the Temple of Skulls at Chichen Itza in Mexico date from around 600 C.E.

AH PUCH, THE DEATH HUNTER

The Maya feared death. They most certainly did not want to end up in the lowest level of the underworld with Ah Puch, god of death.

The Maya were sure they knew how to avoid Ah Puch because he would always give himself away by making a noise as he hunted.

Ah Puch made a big mistake when he killed the head god, Itzamna. When Itzamna came back to life, he banished Ah Puch to darkness in the underworld. Ah Puch dressed as a skeleton and wore an owl head instead of his own. He began to hunt and capture humans to join him in his dark world, but as he came near, he would hoot like an owl. Soon, humans came to fear the sound of a screeching owl as a sign of death. They believed that the only way to save themselves was to moan, groan, and shriek to fool Ah Puch into thinking that they were already being taken by one of the other gods of the underworld.

Left: The Aztec god of the dead was Mitlantecuhtli, shown here in a gold pendant from the 1400s.

THE NATURAL WORLD

Mesoamerican people ate a variety of foods, including vegetables, insects, wild animals, and grains. The most important food was maize, or corn.

Maize was the single most important crop grown in Mesoamerica. It could be eaten fresh or dried and ground into flour. Maize helped to prevent starvation because it could be stored for long periods of time and eaten when other food was scarce.

Squash provided the people with a healthy and easy-to-carry vegetable. It also contained seeds that were full of **nutrients**. Certain types of squashes could also be hollowed out to be used as water bottles.

Beans were often used in cooking. Maize, squash, and beans were the three vital crops known as the "Three Sisters." In the highlands, where the ground was dry, the cactus plant became an important food source. People ate the beetles, flies, grasshoppers, and white worms that lived in them. They also used cacti to make an alcoholic drink called mezcal.

Below: These Aztec farmers are harvesting maize and removing the husks. Maize was the most important food that they ate.

LINK TO TODAY

The method the Maya used to clear ground, called slash and burn, is still employed today. Trees are burned to clear land for farming, but the poor soil means more forests have to be destroyed each year to grow crops.

QUETZALCOATL AND FOOD FOR HUMANS

The story of Quetzalcoatl and the ant explained how certain crops became the food of the people of Mesoamerica.

Quetzalcoatl was pleased with the humans he had made, but he realized that they would need food to eat. One day, he saw a black ant carrying a kernel of maize. He changed himself into an ant and followed the insect to find out where it got the kernel. The ant led him to a mountain with a crack in it. Through the crack Quetzalcoatl saw not only maize but also beans, peppers, and sage. Still an ant, he squeezed in and took a kernel of maize. He carried it back to the humans to plant.

Quetzalcoatl asked the other gods what they should do with the mountain. The other gods said to crack it open, so he did. But this angered Tlaloc, the rain god, who did not think it was a good idea. So he stole the beans, peppers, and sage from the mountain before Quetzalcoatl could get them. Mesoamericans made sacrifices to Tlaloc to ask him to be generous with the food that he stole.

Right: As Lord of the Winds, Quetzalcoatl became a god associated with vegetation and fertility. He is shown here carrying grain. His load consists of five cobs of maize, which is the symbol of the maize goddess.

THE TRICKSTER GOD

Huehuecoyotl, also known as the Old Coyote, was the Aztec trickster god. He was a **shapeshifter** who could transform himself into any type of animal or human, and play pranks and get into all kinds of trouble.

PLANTS AND ANIMALS

Plants and animals were seen as creations of the gods. Myths explained why they needed to be respected and cared for. Many festivals in Mesoamerica involved different types of flowers and animals.

Certain flowers were thought to be **sacred**. The water lily has a beautiful white flower that dancers wore during ceremonies. It may have been eaten or smoked to bring on visions. Images of squash flowers were carved and drawn on **monuments** and jars, most likely because squash played an important part in myths.

Jaguars and spider monkeys lived in the rain forests of Mesoamerica. Artwork often shows the gods taking the shapes of these animals. Jaguars symbolized power and **agility**, while spider monkeys were thought to be early humans transformed by the gods into monkeys. Seashells were also valued and were used as offerings placed around the dead.

Plants and animals played an important role in medicine. Priests boiled and used plant and animal parts in herbal drinks or for baths. They also advised the sick to eat, smoke, or rub in certain mixtures to cure illness. Some of the plants they used were chili peppers, cacao, tobacco, and **agave**.

GOD FEATHERS

The beautiful quetzal bird was considered godlike and was associated with the Feathered Serpent of Mesoamerican myths. Rulers and nobility wore headdresses made from quetzal feathers, linking them to the gods.

Below: During the festival of the jaguar god, boys dressed up as jaguars and other animals. This unique festival combines jaguar worship with modern Christianity.

HUNUAPHU, XBALANQUE, AND THE BAT HOUSE

Squash was considered a special, life-giving food among the Maya. Its place of importance was secured when it helped to save the life of one of the hero twins, Hunuaphu.

The twin gods Hunuaphu and Xbalanque were on their way to the underworld to avenge the death of their father, Hun Hunuaphu, when they spent the night in the Bat House. This was home of the Coati, who were monstrous bats.

The twins knew they had to hide from the Coati until morning. They tried to be patient, but Hunuaphu stuck his head out of a window to see if the Sun was rising. One of the Coati sliced off his head, and it rolled onto the ballcourt of the town. Xbalanque was very sad and called all the Coati together. He told them to bring him their favorite food. The bats brought a squash. Xbalanque carved it into a new head for his brother, so they could continue their journey.

Left: In this carving, a god is emerging from a jaguar's mouth. To the side of the god's head are cobs of corn and snakes. Above the head is a seated man, intertwined with snakes and possibly wearing a rain god headdress.

POPOCATEPETL AND IZTACCIHUATL

Two volcanoes overlook the valley of Mexico in Mesoamerica. The story of Popocatepetl, the Smoking Mountain, and Iztaccihuatl, the Sleeping Woman, explains how these volcanoes came to be.

The chief had a daughter, Iztaccihuatl, who was the most beautiful princess in the land. She fell in love with the young warrior Popocatepetl. Her father agreed to let them marry when Popocatepetl returned from battle.

While he was fighting, another warrior, who was jealous of Popocatepetl, told Iztaccihuatl that her lover had died in the war. Overcome with grief, Iztaccihuatl died of a broken heart. When Popocatepetl returned, he took the dead princess and moved ten hills to make a mountain for her to rest on. He stayed beside her with his torch to watch over her eternal sleep. The gods covered them both with snow and to this day you can see the smoke rise from snow-capped Popocatepetl standing guard over Iztaccihuatl.

Below: Snow caps the volcano of Popocatepetl.

THE NATURAL LANDSCAPE

Every part of the landscape held meaning for the people of Mesoamerica. They believed that mountains were powerful places that were built by the gods. Caves were a gateway to the underworld, and the rivers and streams were pathways.

The limestone that is the foundation for this region is easily **eroded** by water, creating large and deep underground cave systems. The Mesoamericans believed that these cave systems led to the underworld.

People were sometimes buried inside caves to help their journey to the underworld get a fast start. The caves were sometimes the site of sacrifices.

With most of the lowlands covered in thick jungles, rivers became ancient highways that connected towns and villages together.

The ground was also an important source of **natural resources**. Copper, jade, basalt, **obsidian**, and gold were mined and used in jewelry, as decoration, and for trade.

THE NEW CALENDAR

The Aztecs celebrated the start of a new calendar with the New Fire Ceremony. A **procession** would climb Mount Huixachtlan, beside Lake Texcoco, where a man would be sacrificed. Torch runners would carry the new fire to light **hearths** in all the temples to symbolize the new beginning.

Below: Attendants puff gold dust through a tube on to the body of the god El Dorado, while his lords enjoy themselves in a hammock.

21

NATURAL DISASTERS

Life was unpredictable and dangerous for Mesoamericans. Entire villages and farmlands could quickly be destroyed by natural disasters.

The mountains of Mesoamerica were not just soaring piles of rock but active volcanoes. Earthquakes and eruptions rocked the area. The ancient people used myths to explain why the ground beneath their feet rumbled and ash rained down on their heads.

Mesoamericans were desperate to find ways to please their angry gods. Some temples were built to look like

USEFUL ASH

Scientists have found ash in settlements far away from volcanoes. The ash may have been put to a good use. Scientists think the ash helped **fertilize** the poor soil so the Mesoamericans could grow more crops.

a volcano, with steep sides and a chamber at the top for **incense**. They also thought blood sacrifice was necessary. They poked holes in their tongues and collected the blood or made human sacrifices.

Below: An Aztec priest offers the heart taken from a living human victim to the Aztec Sun god and god of war, Huitzilopochtli.

THE GODS OF EARTHQUAKES AND MOUNTAINS

The Mesoamerican region has always been subject to earthquakes. These must have been terrifying events for ancient people. To them, it was the work of destructive gods or monsters.

Vukub-Cakix was a very powerful stone giant who had two sons, Cabrakan and Zipacna. Cabrakan was so strong that he could shake the earth. Zipacna was powerful enough to build and move mountains. Their favorite trick was to build up mountains, then shake them into rubble. This caused no end of trouble for the animals and humans who lived there.

Finally, the gods had had enough. They called on the hero twins, Hunuaphu and Xbalanque, to get rid of Cabrakan and Zipacna. The twins watched them and discovered that they both had a favorite food. The hero twins would use this knowledge to trick them and bring an end to their destruction.

Zipacna liked to eat crabs from an underwater cave. The next time he went there to eat, the twins caused an avalanche of stones to bury him. He was trapped underground. Cabrakan loved roasted bird. The twins made him a roast bird dinner, which Cabrakan devored, not knowing it was poisoned. When he lay gasping on the ground, the twins tied him up and buried him at the bottom of a sacred mountain. Every once in a while he rumbles and shakes as he tries to escape, causing large earthquakes.

Right: Tonatiuh, the Sun god, has a symbol representing an earthquake on his back. According to ancient calculations, it was believed an earthquake would finally end the world.

DAILY LIFE

Mesoamerican society was layered, just like the layers of heaven and the underworld where the gods lived. Kings had the highest status. Other people, like slaves or prisoners, were on the lowest level.

Small kingdoms were ruled by a king who belonged to a noble, or high-ranking, family. The royal family would trace their ancestors back to the gods, proving its claim to the throne. Nobles were paid **tributes** by the common people living in their kingdom. Commoners also had to serve in the military in time of war.

Scribes were very important in Mesoamerican societies because they were responsible for keeping state records and for sharing information through **hieroglyphs**, or picture writing. They often worked closely with the king and priests and had their own special gods.

Traveling merchants, called *pochteca*, had special privileges. Because they traveled long distances, they were able to spread news and important information and often were used as spies.

THEIR OWN BEAUTY

Mesoamericans had different ideas of beauty. They would dangle beads on a string in front of babies' faces to make them go cross-eyed. They would also strap boards to their foreheads to flatten their faces.

Below: Aztec merchants traveled great distances from town to town buying and selling goods.

QUETZALCOATL AND THE BAG OF BONES

**The Aztec people wondered why everyone looked so unique.
They knew it must have been the work of the gods.**

Mictlan was the name of the Aztec underworld, which was ruled over
by a lord and lady.

After the world was destroyed for the fourth time, Quetzalcoatl saw
that the fifth Sun burned bright but that there were no people on Earth.
He went to Mictlan to gather the bones of those that had died so that he
could create new men and women from them.

The underworld was a gloomy place, and after the Lord of Mictlan
had given Quetzalcoatl a bag of bones, Quetzalcoatl was in a hurry
to leave. He began to run but tripped and fell, spilling the bag and
breaking all the bones inside into different sized pieces: long, short,
big, and small. He had no choice but to use these bones, so that is
why humans come in all shapes and sizes.

Below: These three Aztec men all looked different
to one another, thanks to the work of the gods.

THE CALENDAR

Mesoamericans used three different systems for measuring time: the Long Count Calendar, the Divine Calendar, and the Civil Calendar. The Maya were the first to really improve these systems. Later cultures, such as the Aztec and the Toltec, used the same calendar but changed some of the names.

The Long Count Calendar counted the days since the day the Maya believed the world started. Scientists do not agree what date that is but figure it is around September 6, 3114 B.C.E. The Divine Calendar counted two types of weeks. Our week has seven days but one of their weeks had 13 numbered days and the other had 20 days each with different names.

The Civil Calendar was similar to our modern, 365-day calendar. Instead of 12 months, however, it had 18 months called *uinals*. Their months each had 20 days, called *kin*. The five kin left over at the end of each year were considered unlucky days.

MAYAN DAY NAMES

Number	Day name	Approximate meaning
0	*Ahau*	Lord
1	*Imix*	Waterlily
2	*Ik*	Wind
3	*Akbal*	Night
4	*Kan*	Corn
5	*Chicchan*	Snake
6	*Cimi*	Death head
7	*Manik*	Hand
8	*Lamat*	Venus
9	*Muluc*	Water
10	*Oc*	Dog
11	*Chuen*	Frog
12	*Eb*	Skull
13	*Ben*	Corn stalk
14	*Ix*	Jaguar
15	*Men*	Eagle
16	*Cib*	Shell
17	*Caban*	Earth
18	*Etznab*	Flint
19	*Caunac*	Storm cloud

Below: This Aztec calendar stone is often called the Sun Stone because the face in the center is most likely the Aztec god of the Sun.

THE END?

The Long Count Calendar will run out in 2012. Some people think this is a sign that the Maya believed the world would end. Scientists say this is not so and that it only means the beginning of a new long count. In fact, the oldest known calendar has just been discovered in Guatemala and has calculations for almost 7,000 years.

STONE CALENDARS

Some temples, such as Kukulkan's temple at Chichen Itza, were built to represent the calendar by the number of steps, sides, and platforms they had.

Below: This 260-day ritual calendar was used throughout Mesoamerica to predict the future. It shows the Moon goddess in the rainy season.

Above: In this reconstruction of a typical Mayan dwelling, the walls are made of twigs and mud, called wattle and daub, and the roof is thatched.

FAMILY LIFE

Just like the gods and goddesses in their myths, who fell in love, married, and had children, Mesoamerican people valued marriage and families. Young children, parents, and grandparents all lived together in one house.

Huts made of poles, mud, and **thatched** roofs were built next to the farmlands where fathers taught their sons to grow crops and to hunt. Mothers taught their daughters the important skills of cooking, looking after the household, and weaving.

Only the sons of kings and noblemen would go to school. Here, some might be trained as scribes to read and write hieroglyphs. Craftsmen, such as potters and stonemasons, also passed their skills on to their children.

THE SKY ON EARTH

Each Mesoamerican home had a hearth that was laid out like the constellation, or pattern of stars, called Orion. The stones were set on the ground to look like the stars in Orion's belt.

IXMUCANE, GRANDMOTHER OF THE MAYA

Family played an important role in Mayan society. The myth of Ixmucane tells how relatives worked to help one another.

Ixmucane was a Mayan goddess whose son had been killed by the lords of the underworld. One day she was greeted by a young woman named Ixquic, or "Blood Moon," who claimed she was carrying Ixmucane's twin grandchildren. But Ixmucane wanted to test Ixquic before she welcomed her into the family.

Ixmucane gave Ixquic a big net and told her to go out into her field and fill the net with food. Ixquic thought this was an easy task and gladly agreed. When she got to the field, she saw that it had only one plant of wild corn growing in it. She fell to her knees and called on Ixcanil, the goddess of seed, Ixtoq, the goddess of rain, and Ixcacao, the goddess of chocolate, to help her.

The three goddesses came quickly. Ixcanil taught Ixquic how to remove the kernels from the corn and plant them. Ixtoq brought rain to make them sprout and grow quickly. Ixcacao taught her how to tend and harvest the fast-growing corn. Ixquic stood on the low hillside and watched in amazement as the whole field filled with ripening stalks. When they were done, Ixquic gathered up the corn until the net was overflowing. She took her net back to Ixmucane. Seeing the miracle, Ixmucane welcomed Ixquic into the family.

Left: Weaving was just one of the many skills mothers taught their daughters in Mesoamerica.

THE GOD OF PULQUE AND THE DRAGONS

Tepoztecatl was the main god of pulque—an alcoholic beverage—and drinking. He was often shown as a rabbit, an animal the Mesoamericans thought had little sense, much like a drunkard. But he became a hero to the Tlalhuica tribe of the Aztecs.

Each year the nearby city of Xochicalco demanded a sacrifice from the Tlalhuica tribe. This year, the tribe had to offer up an old man to be eaten by a dragon. The Tlalhuica were worried and prayed to many gods to help them, but only one answered their prayers. It was Tepoztecatl, the rabbit god of drunkenness.

The Tlalhuicans were not sure what he could possibly do, but Tepoztecatl was tricky. Being a god, he was able to change himself into a human and disguise himself as an old man. The Tlalhuicans sent him to be sacrificed but Tepoztecatl killed the dragon instead. The Tlalhuicans were free of their yearly sacrifice. To thank the rabbit god, they built a large temple to honor him.

Below: A group of elderly Aztecs smoke and drink pulque.

FESTIVALS AND ENTERTAINMENT

Mesoamerican festivals featured dancing, plays, and music. They were performed in the main **plazas** of towns and watched by large audiences.

Priests would check the Tzolkin, the Divine Calendar, to decide the best dates for festivals. The dances were held to celebrate, prepare for war, or as part of sacrifice rituals. The dancers wore fine costumes decorated with shells, feathers, and headdresses that represented animals, historical figures, or gods. They danced to music made by small copper bells, rattles with shells or beads, and drums.

Theatrical plays retold the myths of the gods or other important historical events.

Above: The Aztecs played a ball game in specially constructed ballcourts.

SILLY RABBITS

Centzon Totochtin means "400 rabbits." These rabbits were the gods of drunkenness. Rabbits were considered silly creatures, which is probably why they were invited to all the parties where people were drinking pulque, an alcoholic drink.

Sometimes the performances were humorous plays or illusions, where the audience was tricked.

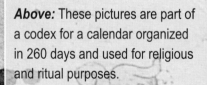

Above: These pictures are part of a codex for a calendar organized in 260 days and used for religious and ritual purposes.

HIEROGLYPHICS

Both the Maya and the Aztecs used hieroglyphic writing. These symbols, cut into stone or written on bark, told of special events or gave information about the kings. While the Aztecs could record some information with their hieroglyphs, it was the Maya who had a complete written language. Many languages today use 26 letters to write. The Maya had more than 800 glyphs, or symbols!

Scribes would use ink and brushes to write on thick pieces of fig bark and then fold up the manuscript, called a **codex**, like an accordion. Only three codices have survived. They are kept in museums in Dresden, Madrid, and Paris. More **permanent** glyphs are found carved into the stone on temples and monuments and tell of heroic deeds of kings and gods.

CRACKING THE CODE

Scientists all around the world worked at cracking the Mayan hieroglyphic code. First, they figured out that dots and lines were used to show numbers. With more study, it became clear that the pictures represented syllables, not single letters like our alphabet. From there, scientists were slowly able to understand the codices and stone carvings.

HUN BATZ AND HUN CHEN, THE MONKEY GODS

Howler monkeys were regarded as gods of the arts. They were musicians, artists, and scribes.

Hun Batz and Hun Chen were the first set of twins born to Hun Hunuaphu. One day, their younger brothers, who would become the hero twins Hunuaphu and Xbalanque, decided to play a trick on them.

Hun Batz and Hun Chen excelled at playing music, drawing, and writing. Hunuaphu and Xbalanque were jealous of the attention given to their older brothers and made a plan to get rid of them. They told Hun Batz and Hun Chen that there were some delicious birds up a certain tree that would make a tasty lunch. Hun Batz and Hun Chen started climbing the tree but could not see the top where the birds were. The higher they climbed, the higher the tree grew. They realized too late that there was no way down. They had turned into monkeys, with their loincloths becoming their tails.

TRADE *AND* WARFARE

Traders and merchants were busy people in ancient Mesoamerica. All types of goods and services were exchanged across the region.

Early Mesoamericans did not have wagons or other **vehicles**. In order to move goods, they ferried loads in dugout canoes on the waterways or had slaves carry huge sacks on their backs. It could be dangerous to travel with expensive goods, so warriors would often escort the group.

One of the most important traded goods was salt. Salt was not only used in cooking to flavor the food but also to

Below: The main market in the Aztec capital, Tenochtitlán, was always busy, with traders selling a wide range of foodstuffs and other goods. The Great Temple can be seen in the background.

preserve meat to keep it from rotting. Salt was produced near the coast by drying large flats of seawater and then bringing the salt inland. Besides food, Mesoamericans also traded jade, obsidian, pottery, jewelry, and furniture.

THE ROYAL STONE

Jade was called the Royal Stone of the Maya. Its green color was connected with the god Quetzalcoatl. It was rare and hard to work with, making it valuable. Jade was carved to make sculptures and jewelry, but also used in armor.

TEZCATLIPOCA PROVES HIS WORTH

The people most prized by the Aztecs were brave warriors. The story of Tezcatlipoca shows that even someone who was thought of as a crazy wildman could earn the respect of the townspeople.

Tezcatlipoca was a wizard and the god of evil. One day, he decided to change himself into a wild, crazy man and wander the marketplace of the town of Tula selling chili peppers.

The king of Tula had a beautiful daughter whom many men wanted to marry, but the king did not consider any of them worthy. The princess saw the chili pepper man and instantly fell in love with him. She pined for him every day until she began to waste away. The king found Tezcatlipoca, cleaned him up, and allowed him to marry his daughter so she would get well. But the townspeople laughed at the king for allowing the marriage. The king was embarrassed and plotted to have his new son-in-law killed. He sent him off to war expecting him to be killed in battle, but Tezcatlipoca was victorious. When he returned, the king and the townspeople praised him.

Tezcatlipoca was given a crown of quetzal feathers and a turquoise shield. The king announced that the chili pepper man was indeed his rightful son-in-law.

Left: Two Aztec craftsmen decorate a shield with beautiful feathers.

THE GODDESS OF CHOCOLATE

Chocolate—made from cacao beans—was so important to the people of Mesoamerica it had its own goddess.

Ixcacao was happy teaching her people how to plant seeds, tend crops, and harvest them. But one day she was whisked away from the fields to marry Ek Chuah, the god of commerce. It was not long before her lovely cacao beans were being used as money. Soon the beans were were available only to nobles.

Ixcacao and Huitaca, the goddess of love and pleasure, thought of a plan. Ixcacao would teach all the kings' cooks how to make the cacao drink intoxicating like wine. Soon everyone was guzzling the drink and becoming drunk. Huitaca was grateful to Ixcacao for helping her bring some pleasure back to the hardworking peasants. To reward her, she covered Ixacao from head to foot with little white flowers.

Below: Chocolate is manufactured from the beans that grow on the cacao tree.

CACAO BEANS AND CHOCOLATE

The cacao bean growing on trees in the rain forest became a valuable and desired product in Mesoamerican society—as it is today. People believed that such a gift must be divine, so they prayed and made offerings to Ixcacao, goddess of chocolate.

The ancient Olmec culture believed the seeds held the secret to health and power. The Maya learned to turn the bitter seeds into a frothy drink called *chocolatl*. This drink was enjoyed by rich and poor, used in ceremonies, and as offerings to the gods, especially Ixcacao.

The Aztecs valued the cacao bean so highly that only the rich could afford it. The beans themselves were used as money to buy other food, clothing, and pots. One cacao bean bought you a large tomato, while 30 got you a small rabbit for supper.

LINK TO TODAY

Just as forgers today produce counterfeit or fake money, the Olmecs faked cacao beans. They took the empty bean shells, filled them with dirt and stuck them back together.

Above: Traditionally dressed Mayan women prepare hot chocolate in their village.

WARFARE

Life in Mesoamerica was a constant struggle for land and resources. As towns and cities grew larger, people turned to warfare to gain more space, food, or goods from neighboring states.

Kingdoms did not have regular armies. If a war was planned, state officials would go from house to house gathering up able-bodied men to fight. Battles would begin on a day picked by priests after consulting their calendars. Scouts would first size up the strength of the enemy's men and forts. Then the army would attack, using their weapons in **hand-to-hand combat**. After the battle was over, the winning army would take prisoners from the losing side. The men, women, and children could become slaves or even be used as human sacrifices.

Right: Huitzilopochtli was the Aztec god of war and the main god of the capital city Tenochtitlán.

WEAPONS OF WAR

Mesoamericans fought with stone clubs, short stabbing spears, axes with blades made of flint or obsidian, blowguns, javelins, and slings. The warriors protected themselves with jade armor or vests stuffed with rock salt.

LINK TO TODAY

The rock salt vests of the Maya were the idea behind today's **flak jackets** worn by soldiers.

Above: Armed with stone clubs and other weapons and protected by their armor, Aztec warriors march into battle against their enemies.

HUITZILOPOCHTLI, GOD OF WAR

Huitzilopochtli was a fierce warrior and legendary wizard. Even before his birth, he began fighting the darkness as a Sun god. Huitzilopochtli was responsible for the creation of the Moon and the stars.

Huitzilopochtli's mother was the goddess Coatlicue, who became pregnant with him when a ball of feathers fell in her lap. His sister, Coyolxauhqui, wanted to kill their mother because of the shameful way she had become pregnant. Huitzilopochtli learned of this plan while he was still in his mother's womb. Before his sister could act, he sprang from his mother's womb fully grown and armed, and killed his sister. She became the Moon so that his mother could be comforted by seeing her every night. He also killed many of his 400 brothers, and they became the stars.

Huitzilopochtli lived in a beautiful palace in heaven. This was the place where warriors who died in battle or women who died in childbirth would spend eternity. Sometimes they would come back to Earth as butterflies or hummingbirds.

MESOAMERICAN LEGACY

Many of the traditions and objects discussed in Mesoamerican myths still exist today. They include temples, music, offerings, and the calendar.

The Maya were famous for their step pyramids. These stone buildings could be up to 165 ft (50 m) high. Each one was dedicated to a different god.

The Aztecs created large, beautiful temples. Their cities often competed with one another to build the most impressive temple. Instead of destroying an old temple, the Aztecs would build the new one on top, making it larger and more complex. Archaeologists have found some temples with four or five layers.

MAKING MUSIC

Mesoamericans used a variety of instruments to make music. Wind instruments, such as flutes, whistles, and **ocarinas**, were made of clay, wood, or bone. Drums and maracas were made mostly from wood and tortoise shells. Pictures on an ancient Mayan pot also show a stringed instrument. When scientists recreated it, they found it made a sound almost exactly like a jaguar's growl.

TONATIUH, THE AZTEC SUN GOD

The Aztecs believed that each time Earth was created and destroyed, a new god became the Sun god. They believed they were living in the fifth Sun. Its myth involved sacrifices.

When it came time for the fifth Sun, the god who used to be called Nanahuatzin took the new name, Tonatiuh. Tonatiuh was very proud of his new position and power. He loved hanging in the sky so much that he did not want to move. He decided that the only way he would make his way across the sky would be if the other gods made a sacrifice to him with their own blood.

The Lord of the Dawn was furious. He shot an arrow at Tonatiuh, but the Sun god caught the arrow and threw it back at him, hitting the Lord of the Dawn in the head and making him cold. That is why the dawn is always chilly. The other gods realized that they were in for trouble if they did not obey, so they cut out their own hearts as a sacrifice to Tonatiuh.

LINK TO TODAY

Modern sacrifices do not involve killing humans or animals. They usually take the form of a period of **fasting**, such as during Muslim Ramadan, or giving up something cherished such as during Christian Lent.

Left: The temples in Teotihuacán in Mexico are almost 2,000 years old. Sacrifices and other offerings to the gods were made on the flat platforms at the top.

41

Below: Led by their god, Huitzilopochtli, Aztec priests discover the spot where an eagle, devouring a serpent, perches on top of a cactus. There they decide to found Tenochtitlán, capital city of the great Aztec nation, in 1325.

PLACE OF THE PRICKLY PEAR CACTUS

The Aztecs had a tradition of fighting with neighboring tribes and so had no friends to help them. The god Huitzilopochtli helped them find a place to settle down and build a city.

The Aztecs roamed the land hunting and gathering food and looking for the special site Huitzilopochtli had described. He told them the place would be marked by an eagle, perched on a cactus and eating a snake.

The Aztecs wandered for 200 years until they came upon such a marker. The eagle on the cactus was found on a small swampy island in the middle of Lake Texcoco. They used grass and mud to build their huts and ate the birds and fish that lived around the island. They learned to pile earth to make artificial islands in the swamp, called *chinampas,* to grow crops. They paddled canoes to get around. They called their city Tenochtitlán, which means "place of the prickly pear cactus." This vast city now lies under modern-day Mexico City.

LINK TO TODAY

Today we eat many of the same kinds of foods the Mesoamericans ate. We enjoy beans, chilli peppers, squashes, avocados, and tomatoes, just as they did. We eat the same tortillas, which are pancakes made out of maize. And, of course, we love chocolate.

Below: An Aztec holy person conducts a *limpia*, or cleansing ceremony, next to the main cathedral in Mexico City. He holds a special incense burner made of clay and decorated with images of the mythological gods.

ART FOR THE GODS

Mesoamerican art was a way for the people to express their beliefs in the myths and gods and their respect for their kings.

Stelae are tall stone monuments, several feet high. The sides are carved, and there is often a round stone in front placed on the ground, like an altar. The images and hieroglyphs usually tell the life story of a great king or the myths of the gods.

Most people had both everyday and ceremonial pots and flasks. They were made of clay and either carved or painted with designs. Most items have images of humans, animals, or mythological creatures on them.

MESOAMERICAN LEGACY

The myths, art, and culture of the ancient Mesoamericans live on in other ways. The same colorful shapes and designs that were woven into cloth long ago are seen today in modern fabrics used for furniture, curtains, carpets, and clothing. The style of drawing found in temples and monuments has influenced many modern artists. The old languages have survived, too. Millions of people speak a form of Mayan or Aztec today. The calendar we use today is similar to the Mayan Civil Calendar.

Today people with Mayan and Aztec ancestors still celebrate festivals. While some names have been changed from the ancient gods to Christian saints, the stories and rituals are very much the same. Day of the Dead celebrations take place every year in Mexico. They began as a month-long Aztec festival honoring the "Lady of the Dead" but were taken over by the Christian Church. Every November 1, family and friends get together to remember the dead.

Right: This modern painting by Mexican artist Diego Rivera uses the bold colors of the Mayan style.

Below: Colorful ceramic skulls for sale in Mexico today are based on Mayan designs.

TIME CHART

11,000 B.C.E. The first hunter-gatherers settle in the Mayan highlands and lowlands

2000 B.C.E. The Olmec civilization grows, from which many aspects of Mayan culture are created

700 B.C.E. Mayan writing develops

400 B.C.E. The earliest known solar calendars are carved in stone

300 B.C.E. The Maya begin to be ruled by kings

100 B.C.E. The city of Teotihuacán is founded and becomes the cultural, religious, and trading center of the region for hundreds of years

100 C.E. Olmec culture starts to decline

500 The city of Tikal becomes a great Mayan city

600 A mysterious event destroys Teotihuacán; Tikal becomes the largest city in Mesoamerica

751 Trade between Mayan areas starts to fall off and conflicts erupt

899 Tikal is abandoned

1200 Northern Mayan cities begin to be abandoned

1325 The Aztecs settle and build the city of Tenochtitlán in Lake Texcoco in central Mexico

1452–1454 Famine kills many people in Tenochtitlán

1510 Severe floods cover Tenochtitlán

1517 The Spanish arrive in Mesoamerica and bring with them diseases such as smallpox, influenza, and measles. Within 100 years, almost 90 percent of the population has died.

1521 Fall of the city of Tenochtitlán as the emperor surrenders to the Spanish

1522 Tenochtitlán is rebuilt as Mexico City, capital of New Spain

GLOSSARY

agave A tough plant with spiny leaves that grows in hot, dry areas

agility Ability to move quickly

ancestor Family member from the past

codex (plural: **codices**) Ancient writings collected in book form

cremate Burn a dead body

drought A long period of no rain

dual Having two sides

elite The very best

erode To eat away by wind, water, or ice

fasting Going without food for a long period

fertilize To add nutrients to the soil

flak jacket A sleeveless jacket worn by soldiers to protect them from bullets

hand-to-hand combat The fighters are very near to one another and not firing weapons from far away

hearth The area in front of a fireplace

hieroglyphs Writing in which pictures represent words, syllables, or ideas

incense Something that is burned for the sweet smell it makes

jade A shade of green; a precious stone

leprosy A disease that damages skin and nerves, causing fingers and toes to deform

limestone A rock laid down as sediment that is easily eroded

monument A statue or structure built to remember famous people or events

natural resource A material used by humans that comes from nature such as water, trees, and minerals

nutrient Something that helps plants and animals grow and be healthy

obsidian A hard, dark volcanic rock

ocarina An ancient flutelike instrument

permanent Lasts forever without changing

plaza A public square or open space

preserve To keep food from spoiling

procession People moving together in one direction

sacred Holy; connected with religion

sacrifice The offering of something precious to a god

scribe A person who reads and records words into a codex or book

scroll A piece of parchment or paper for writing or drawing

shapeshift Able to change appearance

starvation To suffer from hunger

suicide The act of taking one's own life

thatch A roof covered with dried straw to keep the rain out

tribute An amount of valuables paid to show gratitude

tropical Hot and humid climate

underworld A place where the dead go

vehicle Something used for moving objects or people

LEARNING MORE

BOOKS

Dalal, Anita. *Mesoamerican Myths.* New York: Gareth Stevens Publishing, 2010.

Ferguson, Diana. *Tales of the Plumed Serpent: Aztec, Inca, and Mayan Myths.* New York: Collins & Brown, 2000.

Jordan, Shirley. *The Mayan Civilization.* Logan, IA: Perfection Learning, 2000.

Nicholson, Robert. *Aztecs.* New York: Cooper Square Publishing, 2000.

Shuter, Jane. *The Aztecs.* Portsmouth, NH: Heinemann, 2008.

West, David Alexander. *Mesoamerican Myths.* New York: Rosen Publishing, 2005.

WEBSITES

The Mayas for kids
> **http://mayas.mrdonn.org/index.html**

Mayan kids
> **www.mayankids.com**

Mayan culture
> **www.criscenzo.com/jaguarsun/default.htm**

Mayan civilization: videos, lessons, and games
> **www.neok12.com/Maya-Civilization.htm**

Aztec and Mayan mythology
> **http://library.thinkquest.org/08aug/01185/myth.html**

Aztecs for kids
> **http://aztecs.mrdonn.org**

Ancient America from kids past
> **www.kidspast.com/world-history/0260-ancient-america.php**

Cyber sleuth kids
> **http://cybersleuthkids.com/sleuth/History/Ancient_Civilizations/index.htm**

[Website addresses correct at time of printing.]

INDEX